Father, I Pray

PW The Poet

AuthorHouse™
1663 Liberty Drive
Bloomington, IN 47403
www.authorhouse.com
Phone: 1 (800) 839-8640

Published by AuthorHouse 12/05/2018

ISBN: 978-1-5462-4534-6 (sc)
ISBN: 978-1-5462-4535-3 (e)

Library of Congress Control Number: 2018906824

Print information available on the last page.

Any people depicted in stock imagery provided by Getty Images are models,
and such images are being used for illustrative purposes only.
Certain stock imagery © Getty Images.

This book is printed on acid-free paper.

authorHOUSE®

Father, I Pray

Father, I Pray

Father, today I may be just a raindrop; tomorrow make
me the rain, flowing toward my destiny.
I may only be the wind, but if it is your desire, make me
fierce and strong, blowing adversity away.
Take my hand, and lead me away from darkness into the light—yours.
Teach me to love beyond all comprehension as only you can.
Let the pureness of you bathe me in your grace, chasing after faith.
May all these requests be delivered upon the wings of angels, Father, I pray.

I Awaken

I awaken to the morning sun peeking through my window.
I take a breath and rise, feet touching the floor.
Footsteps lead to an open door—
A splash of water on my face, a realization,
For unknown answers linger at the bifurcation of a searching mind.
But this I know: the season is here, and it's changing me.
It is moving me a step closer, with grace and mercy leading the way.
It is expecting me to be a representation of God's love.

I Am He Whom

I am He whom you cannot see; I am He in whom you do not believe.

And yet, just as the desert thirsts for rain, you thirst for relief from pain, love lost, and life.

You call out my name; you bow your head in prayer to that which is not there—me.

As I

As I close my eyes to sleep tonight, I pray with all my might.

I just want to say, to ask: wherever I am running to, will you, can you be there waiting with arms wide open?

Can you lift me up beyond what my mind has conceived—what my expectations for myself are—stepping into your plan for me?

Will you erase the anger and envy that seek to drown me in my discontentment?

Can you take the hurt, the pain, and rock me in your loving arms until the morning light?

In a heart questioning, can you plant a seed sealed with a holy kiss—with love?

Will you help it to grow, changing me into the person you intended me to be?

Will you dry the tears falling from behind this painted smile?

On this night, before I drift off into the land of slumber, may I have just a little bit of grace to let me know all my tomorrows shall be all right?

My Life

May He paint your life and mine with newness to see beyond tomorrow.

May you and I hear whispered words tumbling down from the heavenly shores,

Disturbing the stillness of the night, and speaking of love.

May your passion—your inspiration—stir that which we call faith,

Stepping into, moving from the ordinary to extraordinary,

Turning no into yes, grabbing hold of dreams, releasing them into a destiny waiting—yours.

May the assimilation of His words authenticate and remove any erroneous misconceptions,

For grace shall move you out beyond and bring you back to reality,

To know that the voyage has not ended but just begun,

Guided by the pure light that is He.

May love stemming from a heavenly source explode into splendor beneath every fiery sunset,

Becoming the muse running through your life and mine.

Watching

As I watched it rain, these words filled my heart, my soul:
I have contemplated for hours on end—
Tried to process what was said, what was done—
Regulation of said knowledge still elusive to wisdom,
Speaking through sermons presented, hoping to cultivate minds.
In the silence, words flowed from heavenly sources—
Breathe in, breathe out—everything bathed in His love,
Not surrendering to but relinquishing an erroneous conception.
Above all the voices, above all the tears trying to ostracize the pain,
I have added and subtracted, but still the answer remains elusive.
I then multiplied it by doubt, divided by the resurrection
of a conscience identifying what is true.
This self-realization I state with a sincere heart: Jesus would not—could not—
have done it that way, for He is about and shall always be nothing but love.

Here Am I

Father, here am I—I shall not move, I shall not hide, for your eyes can see.
Father, here am I—broken, humbled before you, for the roads
chosen no longer appeal to me nor bring me joy.
Father, here is the me who used to be quietly sitting, waiting just for you.
Father, I know what they say; I just want to hear what you say.
I don't know why, but something is telling me, something is asking me … cannot explain it.
Father, my soul is gently weeping, seeking; it is waiting for love, needing
Just a touch, a word from you.

Father, Who Art

'Tis not night—no stars align the heavens—but somewhere the curtain of darkness has been
  pulled down, so I lift my voice in prayer.
Father, who art in heaven, we are asking that you reach down and pick us up in your arms of
  love; we are in need of you. How did we get here, when a life born of woman has lost its
  value?

Unexplainable reasons from a mind tormented with anger, with hatred:
Father, someone is crying, someone has a crisis of faith, someone is hurting, someone's soul
  just died a thousand times.
Make your presence known; fill our hearts with compassion, with love, and teach us to value
  life again.
Don't let us drown in despair or anger; reach down and touch us, for you are welcome here,
  Father, we pray.

Lost

*Through all my rationalization, expectation, lost in the
centrifuge of life, pulled out from the vortex by grace;
Awaking, the sun lighting the way to pathways on the other side of the
rainbow, where mercy was saying yes, love was knocking to request
entrance—no choice but to conclude I am lost without you.
Amazing grace, my bread of life, blessed am I.*

They Say

They say I am a made-up story—just a fairy tale.

If so, in the presence of danger, without a resolution,

When sickness invades your body, making itself at home,

When the winds blow and rain falls, destroying everything in its path,

When the churches are filled in the aftermath of tragedy,

When the tears will not cease because the pain is eating a hole in your heart—

Why do you call, why do you whisper my name?

Why are you praying?

Is it because you thought no one was listening?

If I am just a fairy tale, why are you looking for and seeking comfort from the make-believe
person you say I am?

What makes you believe that you are the only beings who exist?

In the vastness of the universe, there are many secrets, but I am not one of them.

Your fairy-tale ending has been and will be rewritten by love.

There Is

There is a cool breeze blowing from the north.

There is a rainbow crossing over majestic mountains reaching up to catch the sunlight.

There is a silence; there is a stillness seeping into the night.

There are tears falling into yesterday, yet paving a path to tomorrow.

There is a sorrow in search of joy.

There is a prayer waiting to be heard, to be answered.

There is a doubt; there is a reason to question but only find answers are still elusive.

There is a heart looking for a lost soul to help.

There is a me and a you in the midst of life, asking to be emptied out,

Wanting more, seeking more but not knowing what, calling

on rationalization to open doors to clarification.

There is a change hovering above the heavens, waiting just for you, for me.

There is a love pouring down like rain; let it bathe you in the fullness of

grace, stepping into strength, ending the search and the questions,

For clarity has found a pathway to change, and a heart is open to possibilities—just love.

The Sun

The sun has disappeared into the sunset, replaced by a blanket of darkness; stars are carefully placed, lighting up the night sky.

The wind gently caressing the leaves on the trees, disturbing the stillness of the night, I offer this prayer.

In the midst of raised voices describing, questioning all that He was,

Seeking, searching to find a resolution, an answer to life—His.

"It's just a fantasy … a made-up fairy tale … offering not a happy ending.

Stories void of truth," they say but forgetting the real story that was told.

In your awakening, your lying down—your tears, your anger, your disbelief, your hurt, your pain—may He yet reveal himself to you and make you aware of His incomprehensible love.

Somewhere

Somewhere the sun is rising; somewhere the sun has set, pulling down a cloak of
darkness with counted stars across the heavens, so I offer this prayer for each:
May your search come to an end, stepping into grace, propelling you onward into change.
May your hunger, your desire for something more, open your eyes to see through His.
May He fill your heart with compassion, erasing contemptuous
thoughts, leaving you standing on a solid rock of love—His.
May joy be yours; may He lift you up beyond expectation of self.
May it be well with your soul to open the door to faith, knocking, finding strength in Him.

Don't

*Don't give away the song He has placed in
your heart; just dance to the melody.
Don't let them take your joy because they let theirs slip away.
Don't see through their eyes, but see through eyes of love—His.
Don't let the words they speak color your world with
untruths; see the rainbow with waiting possibilities.
Let them know your Father knew what it was like to love someone—
you—for He gave of His life unconditionally and unexplainably.
May this love chase after you with each step taken,
with each bated breath, saying always*

Silent Night

Silent night, holy night—all is not right, can humanity save humanity,
or shall we continue to drown in self-hatred for each
Silent night, holy night. Shall anger continue to lead us into an abyss,
chasing after a concept, a truth, left only to our understanding?
Silent night, holy night—shall we each take up arms—protecting
self—only to find when the sun rises no one is left?
Silent night, holy night—a resolution to be prayed for but not at hand, for
the bickering opinions of the many shall overshadow an answer.
Silent night, holy night—despite what you believe or do not believe—who you
pray to or don't—this world is reflecting every color of the rainbow and is slowly
drowning in a vortex of violence. This life we hold dear may soon be no more.
Silent night, holy night—for you may not agree or understand, 'tis the weapon
I know and have is prayer, so I lift my voice for San Bernardino.
Silent night, holy night—like my Father, I choose love.

May You

May you awaken renewed because loving arms held you through the night—His.

May your hurt—your pain—be erased, calling it joy as the sun rises, for the day is new.

May your dreams, your expectations of yourself become a reality.

May the love you seek not be sleeping but waiting just for you.

May every breath taken tell you and help you to see that blessed are thee.

This Night

On this night as the winds caress the leaves, as the moon and stars compete for position,
lighting up the night sky, 'tis time to bow my head; 'tis time to offer this prayer:
Father, who art in heaven, here am I. Here are we, barely holding on.
For we are falling into an abyss of uncertainty fueled by anger, disillusions, chasing after
what we believed to be true but finding no solace in what was said or what was done.
Let us know, open up our hearts to see that in the fullness of your grace, you shall
lift us up into an incomprehensible love gifted freely but with a price: your life.
Whatever you need to do, here are we. Show us, change us,
and help us to love once again. <u>Father,</u> I pray.

Fill Our Hearts

Don't let our hope be drowned by fear. Let us see the light in the midst of darkness.

Don't let doubt get ahead of faith, wondering where you are.

Anger and hatred are saying, "We win once again!"—screaming loudly.

Father do you hear us? Are you listening?

Once again, the innocents have fallen, tearing our hearts apart.

Releasing tears, falling. We stand searching, we stand asking.

Voices raised, fueling their own agenda; we want to hear yours above the rest.

Let not another second or hour pass, for we need thee now.

Father, do you hear us?

Lift us up into thy arms, hold us, and tell us everything shall be all right.

Fill our hearts with compassion and with love. Father, we pray.

Lifting Up

Lifting up my voice this night in prayer,

Calling all angels upon thy wings, deliver these words:

Father, who art in heaven, we have lost our way. We are drowning in despair and anger.

Open our eyes to see love; moving over majestic mountains standing.

For thy kingdom come, thy will shall be done.

Give us strength, Father, strength to reach us in the fullness of thy grace.

Lift us up above all that is to what should be.

Forgive us our mistakes that have led us astray.

Deliver us from all things that seek to redirect our paths

to that which is not pleasing in your eyes.

For thine is the kingdom, the power, the glory, to dwell with thee now and forever.

Let This

Let this be my prayer for you on this day:
I pray you are and shall be all right as the pain and sadness dissipate into the morning sunrise,
     carried away on the wind.
I pray that His grace may guide you to a place of love and a place of joy.
I pray that each step taken leads to serenity, for His mercy says so.
I pray that what hurts you is washed away by
tears falling from angelic eyes.
I pray that you not be hungry nor cold as the
seasons change.
I pray you find your light gifted from above,
showing the way to a waiting destiny, scripted by
     holy hands.
I pray that you are and shall be safe and that
you always find a way through life's obstacles.
I pray that He continues to watch from above,
instilling faith to lost souls seeking.
Let this be my prayer on this day for you.

In Silence

*In the silence of the night beneath the moonlight, in the
stillness of the morning as the sun rises
with dew-kissed flowers reaching up, words tumbling from heavenly shores, delivered
on the wings of angels in answer to a question—a prayer rising from the depths of a soul
saying, yes I would do it again for life, for love, and for you.*

May Your

May your problems quietly slip away into the night.

May your tears erase all the hurt to leave you stepping into joy.

May peace be thine closing the door on turmoil.

May you be loved, and may you matter to someone.

May your dreams become a reality.

May He draw you close never to let you go.

May you come to know and understand like the wind that which you cannot see but feel.

May you feel his love beside you, in front of, and all around you, till time's end.

I Have

I have come from yesterday to tomorrow.
I have come from before to after.
I have come from the behind to the front.
I am no longer past but present.
For like a planted flower blooming into petals falling,
There was love, emanating from a heavenly source.
So the me that I was, I am not—
Changed by grace, kept by His love.

Got My

I awaken to the morning sun peeking through the window,

The sound of birds singing their song as the wind hum along.

Thoughts run through the bifurcation of a mind, speaking to what is, not what was.

Got my eyes to intellectualize the light shining on me.

Got my hands to grasp hold of life propelling me onward into the next realm of reality, which is love.

Got my mouth to speak, telling of the secrets flowing from a heart bathed in grace.

Got my feet to walk into the waiting destiny, scripted by holy hands.

Got my ears to listen attentively, finding comfort in silence, letting words of wisdom change me.

Got each intricate part of me as one to become one with He who is.

Day is Done

Day is done, eyes closing to sleep as the darkness paints the skies.
Off in a distance, I see the moon is awake as it gazes over the earth.
A prayer of sorts escapes my lips as a gentle breeze enters through the window:
Yesterday you may have been in the midst of a storm, but may you be a raindrop in the
tomorrows to come, chasing your destiny, fueled by love stemming from a heavenly source.
As the sun rises on tomorrow, may you know that it is a beginning, an end to what
was yesterday, the pain, the hurt, the anger, replaced with joy, with peace.
And may you know you matter, if not to them but to Him, whose strength and
courage gave a gift no one has or ever will give: His life for love, for you.

Darkness

Darkness has overtaken the daylight as the silence seeps in, unaided by the wind. Eyes search the heavens, wanting, waiting to hear, for yesterday I stood in the midst of grace. Tomorrow, I shall wipe away the raindrops of mercy, chasing after a destiny written by holy hands.

I shan't turn around, for as I step into the unknown—placing footsteps, standing upon maybe nothing, and lead by faith—I shall be taught how to fly, for I am bathed in his love, and for that I say Amen!

If God

If God has put a period at the end of the sentence,
which speaks to mistakes made; words said; tears cried
from a hurt; sorrow chasing after discontent; anger
choking you of your gift of life; and all the whys, what
ifs, and whens, then with a heart full of love speaking
from the heavenly realm, stop trying to erase it, for
in His heart it was forgotten and forgiven before you
stepped through the time continuum and made it so.

'Tis Time

'Tis time to lay head upon pillow, but I offer this prayer:

Father, who art in heaven, hear our cry, our prayer.

We are asking for strength to stand together in faith, chasing after peace.

We are asking for grace to release us into mercy, opening our eyes to see the glory of you.

Erase our fears and wrap us in your arms, for we seek rest.

Infiltrate our hearts and souls with understanding. Let not differences separate us.

Catch our many tears and reassure us everything will be all right.

For we are in need of love. Show us how to once again.

Lord, we need you; not tomorrow, not yesterday, but this

second. We are waiting. Father, I pray.

I Look

I look out the window to find a veil of darkness has been pulled across the night sky, catching
    falling stars in its midst. I bow my head and offer this prayer:

Father, who art in heaven, keep me humble in the presence of many.

Fill my heart with compassion so that I may see through grace-accepting eyes.

Change a prideful heart so that I can hear the lost speaking.

Silent night, holy night—let love be the explanation of my life.

Let me reflect just a little of the pure light that is you—my desire, my request—Father, who art
    in heaven.

I Won't

I won't be regulated to a quiet corner of what we call life.

I shall not be afraid, for my soul will surely not fade;

Shan't drift into a sea of fear because of things unknown;

Won't be held captive by the uncertainty of tomorrow or question where yesterday has gone.

For if I must, I shall enter into heaven's rest, but for now I weep

For those whose breath of life was cruelly taken while sitting, quietly worshipping.

Father, who art in heaven, come sit down with us in the midst of this tragedy.

Make yourself at home in our hearts and release the pain, the hurt,

To be caught, carried upon angel wings, to lie before thee.

Wrap comforting arms around each; where we are now saying, "I can't," let us hear your voice say, "I can, I will, I shall, for I am."

I Pray

The sun is about to rise, to make its presence known, signifying the start of
a new day, but somewhere across oceans of blue waters, there is a blanket of
darkness and stars dancing across the night sky, so I offer this prayer:
I pray that in your awakening, may you be guided with grace-planted footsteps.
I pray that your questions find answers, searching no longer but allowing mercy to speak.
I pray that wisdom makes itself at home in troubling thoughts, relinquishing falling tears.
I pray that you are protected from sorrow and anger,
attempting to find a pathway to your door.
I pray with the innocence of a child that your faith be steadfast
and true through trying circumstances.
I pray that you come to know—to understand—that in arms of love he holds
you. 'Tis the place to be despite the noise heard above the clouds saying no.

On This Night

On this night, as the stars accentuate the night sky, before you close your eyes to sleep, may you always know, may you always believe, that thou art a rare jewel buffed to almost perfection by his grace, his love, and I say blessed are thee.

May You

May your heart be embedded with love reaching out to embrace others.

May you be inspired with courage to see—to understand—the difference.

May peace be the joy waiting to infiltrate a mind in unrest seeking an understanding.

May not a pot of gold at rainbow's end you find but blessings kissed with love.

May your tears, your struggles, and your questions be delivered
upon angel wings to him, laid down and left there.

And may your way be made clear with each step taken, falling into
grace, knowing that you are loved. Father, I pray on this night.

This Night

Father, on this night, as words tumble out in prayer, I plead, can you stay with me?

Can you lift me up above chaos, above the noise of those speaking but saying nothing?

Can you move when I move, from left to right, right to left, front to back?

Can you strengthen me in the presence of adversities, allowing joy, allowing peace to run in?

Can you be the light, piercing the darkness, opening up a newness bathed in grace?

Can you hold me, just not tonight but always?

Can you—will you—just stay with me, bathing me in thy love, asking and saying, "Always."

Let Your

Let your passion move you through life, releasing the fistful of tears you are holding on to, but let God be your passion, releasing you into an unselfish love waiting just for you.

Our Souls

*On this night, Father, move our souls to mercy's seat, to bow down humbly, asking directions to
     the throne of grace,*
Casting our eyes towards heaven, desiring just a sprinkle of thy love.
Hide not, Father. Fill our hearts with you, to feel the sweetness of peace is our desire.
Incline thine ear to hear our prayers, surround us. Bathe us in the glory that is you.
Come, release the darkness from minds in turmoil to the pure light that is you.
Faith seeks no signals from the wind for prayers rising up.
For we know nothing is impossible for you; thou art incomprehensible love in motion.

I Want

I want to be kept in His grace, drowned in His mercy, instilled with unshakable faith and bathed in His love, always.

Printed in the United States
By Bookmasters